BIANCA GOUCH

Beautiful

BETRAYAL

Beautiful Betrayal

By

Bianca Gouch

My Story

Publisher

Victorious Living, Living Victoriously, LLC

Dr. Deborah L. Sheppard

37 Frank Cook Rd. Newnan Ga 30263

Registered with U.S. Copyright Office November 12, 2024

Dedication and Acknowledgments

To God. As I write about the journey and the light that has been bestowed upon me, I thank You. I thank You for the knowledge and strength to "see it through". Thank You for opening my heart and my spiritual sight while dimming the physical distractions. It is my duty and my privilege to carry this assignment, boldly and willingly.

Damian, to you I give my love. I loved you then and I love you now. You have given me the greatest gift, which was unconditional love and a beautiful daughter. Thank you for the lessons that you taught while you were here physically and even more, thank you to the ones that you have taught me spiritually. I will forever hold our memories close to my heart.

Nia, mommy loves you with every breath God loans me. I thank God for choosing me to be the vessel to birth such a beautiful, smart girl. Your eyes tell a story and only a few will understand what I mean. Your soul shines so bright, your spirit so pure that it seeps through your beautiful eyes. You are destined for greatness, and I am so glad that God gave me the opportunity to have a front row seat. I love you, baby girl.

To my sister, you are and have always been my motivation to strive for greatness. I look at you and see not only my sister, but a woman who deserves the world. Your tenacity and strength are evident in all that you do. It is my duty to remind you every day that you are that girl. Thank you for being my best friend and thank you for always being my shoulder lean on, cry on, person to laugh with and most importantly, my light when I struggle to see at time. I love you.

To my parents, you both have done an amazing job when it comes to this parenting role. As I am now a mother, I realize how this is a never-ending job. A role that is given to God's strongest. Mom, you have held my hand and guided me even when I could not see my way at times. Dad, your prayers and talks stay with me even when I cannot physically hear them, they are embedded in my heart and mind. I love you both and appreciate all that you do.

To my best friends, my family and newfound connections. God put you all here for a reason. I cherish the relationships that we share. I pray for continued peace, love, friendship and happiness in all our lives.

Special thanks to, Apostle Dr. Deborah Sheppard. Apostle, you saw in me what I could not see amid the darkness. I was not able to grasp where God was taking me, but you grabbed my hand and guided me. You spoke life into me and for that I am forever grateful.

Prophet Elijah Griggs, thank you for your prayers and spiritual leadership. Your insight and teachings are the reason I am continuing to seek new heights within this spiritual journey.

Table of Contents:

Introduction.. Pg. 6

Introduction

For I know the plans I have for you says the Lord. What if those plans have absolutely nothing to do with what you had hoped for? What if the plans you "thought" God spoke to you were misinterpreted and interrupted, shattered by sudden tragedy? The plan that once was so clear, so sure and solid in your mind was now clouded with doubt and confusion; what seemed like answered prayers now felt like distant memories. Life's unexpected blow feels like a betrayal, leaving us cold and lonely. What seemed like an answered prayer was now only a memory. You can feel the gut-retching punch and slap in the face by life. What was once beautiful turned into a betrayal in the eyes of the weary and heartbroken. The life that you once envisioned was within reach but was taken away before it could fully materialize. The times that were cherished and brought such joy and warmth were now gone, leaving you cold and lonely. What now? How are you to move on from the feelings that are now surging through your body? Mental pain is causing physical pain, paralyzing you from moving forward with life. Yet, the silver lining in this is that you are carrying life literally. A baby needs you. You must pick up the pieces; you must find the strength to continue this journey. You lost a life, yet God is giving you a life at the same time. How ironic? The epitome of "His thoughts are not like our thoughts; His ways are not our ways'. Going from feeling as if God has heard you to "God, where are you?" The questions that arise in the aftermath of tragedy can cloud your spirit and soul. The beauty that emerges from tragedy can only be appreciated when you remember the solid foundation upon which you stand, God. The story of tragedy does not end with a period; it is the start of something more profound, and something more beautiful lies ahead. The challenging aspect is to surrender to God's guidance, even during painful moments, and to open your heart to the journey and the lessons it brings. Embracing the growing pains will help you evolve into the person you are meant to become.

Chapter 1

A Sure Plan

It is one thing to have faith in what you believe God for, but it is something completely different when what you prayed for is staring you in the face. Literally, I can remember writing down my dreams and prayers. As the bible says, write the vision and make it plain. I don't know how much more detail I could get because I was very clear with my vision and prayed to God. Years before writing down the plan I saw for my life, I remember telling God, "I am content." I am content with where I am in life. I had a decent job, a master's degree, and was making decent money; that was clearly enough for just me. I had my apartment and was indeed at peace with where I was, yet I could not deny the fact that I still wanted "my person." Many women in my age bracket or older may say that they are okay with being single, and yes, I am "okay" with it, but I have always desired marriage and family. So, amid my contentment, I still was very clear with God that I wanted my husband. A man that was perfect for me. One that I did not have to question, one that loved me unconditionally, one that made me laugh unexpectedly, and one that made every day feel as though it was a mini vacation. My God-sent man. I was willing to be patient and not rush God's timing, so I enjoyed being single. My best friend would say that we had a time the summer before my "God-sent" man, and I can truly attest to this statement. I have always believed in God's divine timing, yet this stage in my life really brought to light how God truly placed people in your path at the right place and the right time.

On a random homecoming night at my beloved Alma Mater, Fort Valley State University, at the Old School Jam hosted by the Omegas, I was met with fate. I can remember vividly sitting at a designated table with my friends and cousin. I had on a black romper, hair in braids, black open-toe shoes, and red lipstick. As we were laughing and talking, this Omega came over and asked if we needed anything, and specifically looked at me and asked if I would like a drink. I politely declined because, honestly, I do not oblige in drinks that are brought to me by other people, especially someone I do not know. A few moments later, this same Omega asked if we would like a group picture. My group and I obliged and allowed him to take our picture. The party continued, and we enjoyed ourselves and stayed until the end. As I was sitting at the table waiting for my friend to finish her dance and talk with this guy she was interested in, the Omega that asked if I wanted a drink and that took our group photo walked over to where I was sitting, and we began conversing. We talked about so much, and the conversation just flowed. By the end of the conversation, he asked, "How can I get to know Bianca more"? I was enjoying his conversation so much that I did not hesitate to give him my number. It was such a breath of fresh air to have someone who was such a gentleman and was able to carry on a mature conversation. He was interested in me and did what I had not seen in so long. He walked up to me and had a genuine conversation. He was very consistent with his task of getting to know me more, yet I did not initially return that consistency. I was not ready to completely commit due to being hurt so many times before. I was enjoying my single life, yet I remembered it by praying to God. What if this was my person, finally? I had to give it a chance, at least, so I did. The. Best. Decision. I. Made.

Damian. He stood out from so many because of his intentionality. I can remember him scheduling our first phone call. Yes, he scheduled a phone call. The day before, he asked me if I would be available the following day for a 4:00 pm phone call. I was very eager to talk with him and could not wait. On that day, he called me at 3:15 pm and let me know that because he and his brother were running behind on detailing a car, he would be late for our 4:00 pm phone call. I am floored. Who is this man? I couldn't remember a man following through on planning an actual date, yet this man was letting me know he would be late for a phone call. Who does this? The man you prayed for, that's who. That evening, we stayed on the phone for 4 straight hours with no silence. I was catching up with a long-lost friend that I had not talked with in years. There was no dull moment during that phone conversation.

For our first date, he sent an invitation through Eventbrite with the date, time, and details of when he would be at my apartment to pick me up. He explained to dress comfortably. In my head, at this point, I am truly thinking, "This man is too good to be true." We went to Rigsby Entertainment Complex and had a blast. We bowled, ate pizza, played arcade games, and got to know each other well. After the date, we got back to my apartment, sat in the car, and talked some more. I loved that he loved music just as much as I did, and it made it even better that we both loved Anita Baker. He played "I Apologize," and it was the most peaceful after-date car date ever. He looked over at me and asked me if I would like to dance. I wasn't sure if he was serious, but I replied yes anyway. Before I knew it, he had walked around to the passenger side door and asked for my hand. We danced, with the music playing as loud as it could go to Anita Baker in my apartment complex parking lot. I knew then. I just knew.

From that day forward, there was no doubt in my mind that God had sent this man to be a part of my life. There goes one of those pointers that I mentioned in my prayer: I wanted to be sure, without a doubt. I checked that off my list. I can remember us falling in love together. To me, it seemed so quick, so I never wanted to say the actual words, and neither did he. We would say statements such as "I love July 7" or "I love December 20," which were our birthdays. One day, as we were leaving Riverside crossing to do some shopping, I decided to make the first move and tell him that I loved him. He was not "legit" my boyfriend yet, as we had not made anything official. One day, while at my apartment, he asked, "Would you do me the honor of being my girlfriend"? Now, due to being in relationships in the past, I never had anyone officially ask me to be their girlfriend. I can remember having to ask the question, "What are we?" This was just another box checked. This man never kept me guessing; it was the sense of security that I received from him that made me slowly begin to melt into the feminine, submissive woman that I believe every woman should feel comfortable being. I never had to question him, which made it very easy for me to follow. He was a true leader.

Damian ensured that there was always a "we." He truly wanted to know how I was throughout my day—calling me, texting me, and facetiming. The effort that he put into our relationship was so remarkable. I remember our first Valentine's Day. On Valentine's Day morning, he texted me and told me that he would be at my house directly after work to pick me up at 8 pm sharp. I did not already have an outfit, but I had so many options that I would go to the mall and find some shoes that would go with a dress that I already had. When I got back to my apartment, I rushed to my room to begin getting dressed because I knew the time would pass, and it would be 8p before I knew it. As I walk into my bedroom, I am shocked. I had a handmade basket with my name on it, filled with all my favorite items. I have a Ralph Lauren purple dress and some Jessica Simpson heels waiting for me, with a letter that was written to me. The letter brought tears to my eyes, and I honestly could not thank God enough for sending me a man who, indeed, was all that I prayed for. That night, we enjoyed spending time with each other, and once again, I knew. I just knew.

Being with Damian was such a joy. We had picnics together, took walks together, randomly went driving on weekends, and just talked during car rides. We took trips together and randomly made a date out of anything. We loved massages, and we would book them or give them to each other. I truly enjoyed planning outings for him and doing spa days for him. He was a sucker for a good foot or back rub. I would randomly give him beard treatments and facials that I looked up on beauty websites or YouTube channels. I loved to take him out on dates as well. We believed in loving each other completely, and it was never one-sided. He took me on trips, and I did the same for him. For his 30th birthday, I made it my duty to make it the best birthday ever. I booked a stay for us at Belamere Suites in Cummings, Georgia. We enjoyed the heated pool, the room service, and the solace of spending quality time together. I took him to dinner and presented him with an engraved watch that had a special message. That same week, we went to Alabama, where we met his sisters and twin brother. He and his brother love the casino, so it was only fitting that we go for their birthday.

For my 30th birthday, he took me to St. Marteen, and a time was indeed had. This man listens to me, and that has made life so much better. Even though the trips and fancy dates were always excellent, some of my fondest memories were simply him randomly texting me, "Can I pick you up for an ice cream date after work", or him coming in from work being so excited to see me as if we had not just seen each other that morning. It was indeed a fairytale. The way he adored me and would always say randomly to family members and friends, "My girl looks good, doesn't she?" always made me blush. We were friends, and that is what truly made our relationship so great. We could talk for hours as if we did not see each other every day. Literally, there was never a dull moment. Going to the grocery store with someone becomes a fun outing; that is when you know you have found your person. We literally used to have fun going to the grocery store on the weekend.

When I had stressful events going on at work or just in life in general, going home and being able to be with him erased all worry; he always instilled peace and led with, "We will figure it out."

When you have someone who lets you know that you are not in this world to figure it out on your own, it is truly a great feeling. Not only were these words from him, but he always followed through with action.

On September 19, 2022, we found out that our lives would change forever. We had discussed that my menstrual had not visited me lately, and it was not out of the ordinary for it to be irregular. My girl always had a mind of her own. This time was different, though, and something told me to take precautions. I told Damian I would take a pregnancy test that day when he got home from work. I could not wait, so I decided to take the test without him. I heard him enter the house about 20 minutes later. I told him to come into the bedroom and that I wanted him to look at the test on the bathroom sink. He went into the bathroom, used that bathroom first, and then walked over to the sink to glance at the results on the stick. He looked up at me with a smirk. There was a "YES" clear as day. We both sat on the side of our whirlpool, me on his lap. He looked at me and said, "We got this". Never did I question those words because when did he "not" have us?

We decided to tell my sister and his twin brother. We wanted to wait to tell everyone else after my first trimester. His twin was so in shock that he did not believe us at first, but once he grasped the fact that we were, in fact, pregnant, he became just as excited. Damian and his brother led us into prayer for a healthy and safe pregnancy. I was so in awe at home. I had a man who always "Led" but not just led; he led with God at the forefront.

We had our first doctor's appointment and found out that I was very early but that there was indeed a little person growing inside of me. Damian was the epitome of "support". He went to EVERY appointment, asked more questions than I did, and read so many books. He would have us read a chapter a night regarding the growth of our baby and what I should expect each week.

One day during work, he asked, "Can I take my girls out for dinner?". That night at dinner, I remember glancing over at him and saying in my head, "This is my life, my husband, and the father of my daughter." I was so content, so happy, so thankful. I smiled to myself and said, "God you answered my Prayer".

Chapter 2

Cracked Foundation

Everything was falling into place; every prayer was being answered. There were literally no signs of things slowing down. We had all that we could ask for. We had each other, a baby on the way that was growing and thriving as she should. My pregnancy was going so well. I had no morning sickness, no issues or feelings of being "pregnant". The only symptom I had was fatigue, and I wanted to nap constantly.

What is it like to be God's favorite? Well, at this time, I would say, look at me. Damian was the perfect partner who was always so encouraging and never complained he cooked dinner every night, the constant belly rubs and foot rubs. He never missed a morning to pray over us and never forgot to give us a morning kiss before work. It was routine, and to us, without it, our day would not go as planned. We still had not told our families that I was expecting yet. We planned to talk to them on Christmas Eve as a whole. At this time, the only people who knew were my sister, his brother, and my best friend.

We decided to do a reveal video and hired a videographer to help capture the moment. We would show everyone on Christmas Eve and post it for the rest of our family and friends to see and celebrate with us via social media. At this point, I was showing it for 4 months, so the video turned out so lovely. All our family was there on Christmas Eve. I had to wear loose clothing so that I did not show as much. It was not hard to hide, yet you could see that I had put on some weight. My face showed it. When it was time to say the grace before we indulged in dinner. Damian and I, along with the rest of the family, gathered around, and Damian led us in prayer. As he prayed and blessed the food, towards the end of the prayer, he stated, "And God, please continue to guide Bianca and me as we continue on this journey of parenthood." The entire room gasped. There were hugs and a lot of happy tears.

Honestly, life could not get better in my eyes. Little did I know it would not get better, yet the opposite was on the horizon.

Shortly after celebrating yet another wonderful Valentine's Day together, on February 22, 2023, Damian came home from work along with his brother. We were going to eat dinner together. The three of us were often together, and you might as well say that Damian's brother was legit my brother as well because we did a lot together. He was often there with us, and this particular night, I am honestly glad he was.

Damian came in and greeted me with a hug and kiss as usual and went to the bedroom. I followed him, and we talked briefly about our day. I was currently working from home, so I told him about how I needed to purchase a new computer soon. In true

Damian fashion, he said, "I will start researching and getting you the best one that you need. No worries." He mentioned that he was tired, and he equated it to him just leaving the gym. He even joked at how his legs were sore and mimicked the walk of a penguin as I laughed. I told him that since he was tired, I would cook dinner tonight, but he insisted that he would. I told him that maybe he should go ahead and take his shower, and after dinner, he could go straight to bed. He agreed but decided to go ahead at least and season the salmon first. My best friend and I were texting, and she was excited that she had paid off her Jeep. I told Damian, and he told me to tell her to come over so we could celebrate. When she got there, he poured her a drink and told her to sit down and enjoy the joys of not having a car payment anymore. He sat down with us, and we began to talk and laugh as we would usually do. Damian looked over at me and stated that he knew I was hungry, so he got up to finish dinner. My friend and I continued to laugh and talk. As we were talking in the living area, I could see Damian in the kitchen. I noticed that he kept looking at his Apple watch. He looked back at me, and we made eye contact. I asked him if he was okay, and he stated that his heart rate was acting weird and was going up. He told me he would be fine, and he walked to the back where his brother was. Within a matter of 5 minutes, I heard his brother yell his name along with a loud "boom." I ran to the back where they were and saw Damian on the floor. I slid on the floor where he was, not thinking about my current condition of being over 5 months pregnant at this time. I put my hand on his face and kept calling his name. My best friend told me to get up off the floor, all while calling 911 for us. She walked with me outside as she saw how upset I was and tried to get me to calm down and be mindful that I was carrying my baby. I tried to calm myself as best as I could, but I had this feeling that I could not shake. I went to the only other option that I knew of at that time. I ran back into the house, grabbed my cell, and called Daddy. "Daddy, I need you to pray really hard; please pray really hard," I told my daddy I was scared, and that Damian had passed out and was not responding. He told me it would be okay and that he was on his way.

By this time, the ambulance had arrived, and they were working on Damian. They had brought him out of the house and placed him in the back of the ambulance. His brother stood at the back, outside of the ambulance. My sister came to my house and tried to get into the ambulance. Because she was a registered nurse, she was hoping that she could assist in any way, but they would not allow her. She ran into the house where I was and just hugged me. I was in a daze at this point because, God, what are You doing?

My mom and a few other family members had arrived at my house at that time, and the ambulance had taken Damian to the hospital. I was lying in my bed, with my mom at the foot of it. We were all waiting for them to call and say that everything was okay, and that Damian would be fine. Soon, my dad called my mom, and I knew from her face that, in fact, everything was not okay. She looked at me and stated, "He passed". My world stopped. I skipped sadness and went straight into anger because, God, how could you do this?". This was so unfair. I had never been so angry in my life. I cursed, I cried, and I couldn't care less about what anyone thought of me. I had no respect for the ones around me, not even my mother. I cursed to no end. My mom asked if I wanted to go to the hospital. I told her yes.

When we arrived, I was still in such a daze, but when I saw everyone there, it hit me. Damian literally was no longer here. He had died. All that was left was a body. I could no longer speak to him, hear his laugh, discuss life with him, plan with him. There would be no more morning talks about what we would do this weekend. Most importantly, I was now a single mother. My daughter no longer had a dad. The only question and statement I could get out was the first one to my mom, "Ma, what am I going to do?" and the second question to myself and whoever could point me in the direction, "I want to see Damian, I need to see Damian." As I walked into the room where his body lay, covered from the waist down with a white sheet, I saw my favorite person. The man that, at one point, I had no doubt would be my husband.

I walked over and could only pull up a chair and sit next to him in silence. I silently cried and eventually put my head on his chest like I would so many times before. What used to be my warm, safe place was now cold and lifeless. God, there is no way you did this to me. This is all I kept repeating in my mind.

As I rubbed my belly, I said aloud, "I am so sorry, Nia." Nia is the name we decided on together for our daughter. She now would never see her father, her daddy, the best person in the world. In my eyes, he was literally the best person. Oh, how I wanted Nia to meet her daddy. He was such a great daddy even before she was even born, and I wanted her to experience this love. As I walked out of the hospital that night with my mom by my side, I came home to a home that would never be the same. I lay in bed and cried.

The journey was beginning. The journey started with so much loneliness, sadness, anger, confusion, and a search for answers. I needed God to tell me something, because none of this made sense. How could you answer a prayer only to snatch it away as soon as it was at its peak? This was so harsh, so cruel. Not only did you do this to me, but everyone associated with me—Damian's family, my family, and most importantly, our daughter. I now had to literally pick up the pieces for what felt like a broken life, a broken foundation that we had started together.

Now, at my OBGYN appointments, I no longer had my partner, the love of my life, with me, holding my hand and asking questions that I forgot to ask. I was so thankful for my mom, but it was still different. I wanted my person. The one that I had built this life with and started this journey with. I wanted my family. The one that was so close to being a family of 3 was now only the two of us.

Damian was laid to rest on March 4, 2022. I was able to speak at his celebration. I remember seeing him for the last time. To this day, saying "for the last time" is surreal. My person. It was such a hard pill to swallow. The anger and emptiness that was felt in the days ahead were almost unbearable. I was so hurt, and I know that wounds that I had bled unto the ones that I was closest to, mainly my mom. I knew that she was one person who was there to help me, yet she could never understand the pain I was in. I was so hurt, mentally and physically. The pain mentally was so bad that I legit felt it physically. I would be so drained, so tired that I felt sick. I wanted to explain this to the people around me, but it felt as though they did not understand it. This led me to shutting down even more. I had nothing to give. Honestly, the only person that kept me going was Nia. I knew I had to be here for her. I had to push through.

I began to seek some solace, peace, and understanding, and the one person I remembered who had all the answers was God. I never lost my belief in Him, yet my faith in His promises was shaken. I needed answers, and I needed to feel some peace. "God, I need you to help me through this." those were the first words I wrote as I began this journey of journaling my prayers and my questions to God. I also began going to therapy, which was slightly helpful, yet I felt as though I needed more. Who I truly needed answers from was God. I was familiar with the 5 stages of grief; it was literally something I taught on a regular basis in my field of study. I knew this. I needed more, something deeper. What I was going through was spiritual. I knew this early on, yet I did not fully understand it yet. I remember my best friend randomly giving me a book to read called "Conversations with God." I started reading it when I went to the park with her one day to decompress and get out of the house. This book was the start of opening my eyes to a more spiritual aspect of life and my relationship with God.

I was hungry for answers, and I needed to know more about what was going on in my life. I wrote God so much, and not only did I write him, but I wrote Damian as well. I needed to feel still as if I had some connection to him. I kept him updated on Nia, our appointments, and how I was feeling. I continued to write to him about how I felt about him "leaving." I remember one particular night I was sitting in my living area in the dark. I began to write to God. In the midst of my writing, towards the middle or end, I got this sporadic thought that popped into my head, almost like an answer to a question that I had been asking God. I wrote down, "You will see Damian again; he may not look the same, but you will see him again." It was so sporadic, and I was not sure if this was just what I "wanted," so I wrote it, but it made me feel better. I charged it to this, which was just a random thought, and left it at that. Deep down, it did feel like something more, but how could that even be? I soon would continue to get more "random thoughts" when I wrote or talked with God. My issue was, is this God, or are these my thoughts?

I continued to pray and continued to write. The more I prayed and the more I wrote, the more random thoughts and the more random "people" would start to come into my life. The more random songs, podcasts, sermons, and even TikTok videos would "relate" or say something that answered a question I had or related to what was going on. Again, this is such a coincidence, and it was helpful during this time. I began to listen and go to Fellowship Baptist Bible, where Pastor Tolan Morgan was the preacher. The sermons were so "convicting," and it seemed as though God was talking directly at me. I could not fathom how these sermons were almost identical to what I had or would "write" to God. The questions I would ask or even thoughts I would have would be answered during a sermon.

I continued to be hungry for spiritual guidance and soon reached out to an old friend who I knew had some connections with spiritual leaders. I needed to continue this journey; something was leading me to it. I had to continue this journey of healing, and the only way I could do that was to dive deeper into who God indeed was and how He was going to get me through this. Again, I had built a foundation on faith and God. This situation just caused me to find out that I had a few cracks, and any type of situation could cause the devil to find his way in. The loss of Damian did that, or at least this situation "tried" to make me lose faith and demolish the foundation I had. What I soon realized was that the loss of Damian would open my eyes to so much more. The loss of Damian may have been the devil's way of hurting me, yet God had bigger plans.

Chapter 3

Remodeling Faith

Growth always comes with pain. I realized that. There is a difference between hearing a saying often and understanding it and then actually having to live with what is being listened to. I have always known this, yet I never truly "knew" what it meant to have to grow through pain. You hear the analogy often; you know that even physically, to get stronger, you must lift weights in the gym; you must work out and continue to increase your endurance. Yes, this makes sense. Yet, when it comes to the spirit, who has really sat down and said, "God, bring on the weight so that I can get stronger in You?" I know I haven't.

Yes, I have dealt with small trials, such as praying that I pass an end-of-the-year test to go to the next grade or praying that I pass a final in college because I needed it to keep a certain grade point average. As I got older, yes, I have dealt with the death of family members. My grandmother passed away on Valentine's Day in 2012 while I was a sophomore in college. I can remember I had a final that day. I had to go to class; there was no other option. She had passed early that morning, around 3 am-4 am. I sat in my car and meditated before going in. Even then, I had a relationship with God, and it was second nature to lean on Him and believe in Him during this time. The difference in this was that I was "hurt," but I did not feel broken. My life lost a piece of what it was, but it wasn't or did not seem as if it was a promise broken. God never said that my grandmother would live forever. She was diagnosed with cancer, and we were also given a timeframe that she would be with us by her doctors, and God gave her years past that. The death of my grandmother did not feel as if it was a pop quiz. It did not sneak up on me; I was preparing for it. So, yes, I am sure this situation made me utilize my faith and lean on God because I did, yet it was not one of those tests that felt "unfair" or unbearable. As I look back, this was level one of getting to the spiritual level I needed at that time. As life continued, each level became more complicated.

In 2019, my daddy became ill. I remember him being in the hospital for a month. He could not walk, and I had never seen my daddy this way. A man that I leaned on for a lot. *Read that sentence again.* I did not see it then, but God was slowly yet surely trying to get me to depend on Him solely. I see it now as I go through this journey of spiritual growth. With this situation, it was "out of the blue"; this was different than the death of my grandmother. I truly needed God to make a way this time because I needed my daddy well. I needed him to get out of the hospital and be better. I had to have more faith in God during this test than I did with the death of my grandmother. This was my daddy; life was different and slightly unbearable with him being ill. I watched my mom go through so much, and I truly needed God to heal my daddy. Yet, my faith was never truly shaken to the point where I felt as if God was "failing me." My dad was still here, and I was seeing progress. When you can "see," it makes having faith and trust in God easier. Now, as I look back on that, I wonder if that really was faith. It was not. Hebrews 11:1 says, "Now faith is the assurance of things hoped for, the conviction of things NOT seen."

This time in my life was level 2 of my spiritual growth journey. God was slowly, yet indeed, showing me that I needed to lean on Him completely. He began to teach me how life gives us some problems that are out of our control, and we need to release that control and allow Him to guide us. I was learning that the opposite of faith was not always necessarily doubt but control. Control was one thing I struggled with. When life did not seem as if it was going as "I" had planned, I became flustered.

In 2020, here comes COVID. We all had to surrender control. You wanted to control everything, yet we had no idea what was going on. As a believer, I had to trust that God would keep my family safe and keep us here. I had to trust that God would take care of us financially, despite the rumors of jobs laying off and the issues with not being able to go to work. I was laid off from my job at that time, yet God provided and allowed me to find another job. There were so many people dying around us, and my anxiety was at an all-time high. I did not want my parents to get COVID because they said that it was detrimental to their population and age group. I was surrendering all control and having to depend solely on God to keep us safe and healthy—level 3. The pandemic taught me on a more profound and higher level how when you do not know what to do, you know who can. God. No one had control over this pandemic. Many people thought they had it figured out, only to learn that they did not. Every aspect of our lives changed during the pandemic. We had to "be still" and get rid of all distractions.

Listen, these two levels, Level 2 and Level 3, were times of testing and building my faith. These two tests had a common denominator in all of them that honestly kept me sane. Damian. I know God was within me as well, of course, but during this time, I was operating more in my flesh and not spirit. I can say this now, but I did not know that then. Every time I felt sad, needed encouragement, needed to feel peace, warmth, and a sense of "keep going," I thought about Damian, and I went to Damian. He was my encourager, and I often went to him before I went to prayer.

Even though I prayed, I prayed and often still needed confirmation. Guess who gave me that confirmation. Yes, Damian. I needed physical confirmation, meaning if I am being completely transparent, I needed it from someone who I could see. Who I could "hear" and who was "physically" present in my life. During that time, I did not have to seek God's voice as much. I was content with the relationship that I had with Him, which was praying and going to church. I believed and worshipped Him, but had I really, truly had to lean on Him completely? The answer is no. I had someone to go to. I was not forced to search for a deeper, more intimate relationship with HIM.

Level 4 of rebuilding my faith slapped me in the face and punched me in the stomach on February 22, 2023. I lost Damian. I lost the one person who I went to and who gave me peace amid chaos. He was there when I was going through the sickness of my daddy. He was there amid COVID-19, making the situation better in so many ways. We quarantined together; he never had me worry about finances because we were in this together. We held each other up. He encouraged me during my time of anxiety with worrying and wanting my parents to stay free of COVID or even us catching COVID. Damian was there. I leaned on him, and in that, all trials were made less and were not as heavy to carry.

What was I to do now? That person was no longer here. What do I do in this situation? What do I do when I am going through the loss of my partner, the love of my life, and father to my child so unexpectedly and literally no one understands? I have support, but no one understands or can tell me how to navigate my life now. I have my mother, yet she cannot help me navigate this grief. I have my daddy, yet he cannot help me navigate this grief. I have my sister, yet she cannot help me navigate this grief. What I learned in this stage of my life was that I was disconnected from God. I was not completely connected or in tune with who HE truly wanted to be to us. He wants to be the one we go to. He wants to be intimate with us. I did not have an intimate relationship with Him. I could not hear His voice because I was not genuinely seeking His voice. I did not have to. I did not need to.

After the death of Damian, I needed answers. I needed to hear God's voice. He needed to let me know what He was doing. I was desperate. I have never had to lean solely on God until now. There was no one else to turn to. I could not turn to anyone else. The emptiness I was feeling was because I had not allowed Him to feel my heart completely. I let my flesh be in control, and that left my spirit hungry. Damian's death awakened my soul. I was forced to move flesh aside and bring forth my spirit. I needed to get to God. I needed to hear him. The only way I was going to listen to Him was if I allowed my spirit to heighten, to grow, to increase. I began to read more, study more, listen more. I searched for God everywhere and in everything. I even started to search for Him in the presence of the sadness I was in. In the death of Damian, I searched for the beauty of God. When I allowed God to triumph over all negatives, I began to grow so much. My eyes, heart, mind, and soul were opened. My faith began to grow like no other. I made it my mission to build my relationship with God and no longer give Him only part of me. I concluded that I wanted to be more than a Christian, a churchgoer who only went to church, worshipped, and quoted scriptures that I heard often. I began to search my soul for what God wanted me to know and learn. Church became more than Sunday morning service. I needed soul restoration. I needed deliverance, and I needed to see the root of what spirituality is and how deep it truly is. I realized that I had only been given the base, the bare minimum. Everything is spiritual, and I wanted to know more. I wanted and craved to understand what a lot of churches "skip" over in church. It is all good to go to church and get a sermon preached or taught to you, but what if you are only getting that and nothing else? What if you are not being taught just how much you are lacking by only receiving the basis of what God can and will do through you?

I am not the same person I was before Damian's death. I began to rebuild. I started to search, and I honestly found it. I no longer stayed at the surface. I realized that God had so much more in store for me, and I wanted it all. I no longer wanted to sit and wonder, I wanted to know. I remember praying to God and asking him to give me "knowing." God, allow me to know and guide me in the way that you want me to go. I need you to help me surrender to Your will. This was the beginning of a new level of faith.

Chapter 4

Undeserved Favor: Grace

As I turned over this new leaf and began this new chapter in my life, I wanted to ensure that God was at the center of it all. I was now a mother to the most beautiful little girl. Nia, meaning purpose. I knew my daughter had a purpose, and she was my purpose and my reason. God blessed me with a daughter so unique and radiant that when I look at her, all I see is God's grace. He is a gracious God who provides us with what we need at the right time, in HIS timing.

While I was in labor, I could not help but think of how I wished Damian was with me. I was so fortunate to have my family there with me, and I knew that I needed to be grateful for what God had allowed. He allowed me to become a mother. When I look back, this was a part of my prayer, the vision that I wrote down years ago. Sometimes, we often forget that just because God does not answer our prayers the way we want HIM to, He still fulfills His promises. They may not come in the way we "thought," yet He is still answering prayers. I was so blinded by what I did not have that I often forgot about what God had allowed. He allowed me to become what I always prayed to be—a mother. Not only did I become a mother, but I birthed a child that was healthy and beautiful, and that filled my heart with so much joy in the midst of a time that was filled with so much hurt and loss.

We do not get to choose how God answers our prayers, nor when or how releasing that control. This is the lesson that I continue to remind myself. God proves Himself to be gracious in so many aspects of our lives, but we must be willing to release what we feel our lives should be. What gives us the right or the authority to believe that we know better than God what is best for us? The audacity of us to even question His will. The one who created us, who knew us before we were placed in our mother's womb.

Being a mother reminds me so much of how God loves us, how He loves me. During this season of hurt, loss, confusion, and anger, I did not understand how God could love me. How could a God who loves me hurt me? How could a God that was gracious cause so much pain and heartbreak to take place?

While listening to Megan Ashley's podcast, *In Totality,* during an episode with Preston Morrison, he stated, *"God doesn't cause the suffering; he redeems the suffering. He uses the suffering".* He went on to say, *"We live in a fallen world; the second man chose to sin."* Suffering is inevitable in this world, and what we have to learn is how to allow God to be God in the midst of suffering. Psalm 34:18 says, "The Lord is close to the brokenhearted and saves those who are crushed in spirit." The verse continues, "he protects all his bones; not one of them will be broken."

The revelation of Psalm 34, verse 18 opened my eyes so much. I realized that God did not do this to me, yet He is using this to bring me closer to Him. To redeem, to guide, to love, and most importantly, to teach me how to continue to allow Him close to me to carry this weight, to protect me, and to help me heal. I would have never been this desperate to know Him more, feel Him more, and be this deep in the word and spirit without losing Damian. Pain forces the believer to search for God in unique ways. I literally had nowhere else to turn. It reminded me of how the devil asked God for permission to attack Job. God allowed it, but He was there the entire time. Job stayed close to God; he continued to trust and believe and never cursed God. Regardless of how angry and hurt I was with God during this season, I still sought God. Even though I was furious, I questioned, I was confused, and I accused God of failing and breaking a promise, but I still sought HIM. God does not expect us to be perfect, as our flesh is far from it. Yet, God only wants us to seek Him. How gracious is He? Despite my anger, despite my doubting, He still covered me and answered each question I had. All I had to do was continue to seek and listen.

The most critical piece in all of this that I continue to repeat is He. STILL. COVERED. ME.

Now, I am a mother; I must protect my daughter and ensure that she can eventually be in this world with the knowledge to navigate all that comes her way. Very similar to the way God is to us.

God teaches us and has left us a roadmap that will help guide us in this life. The Bible was left for us to utilize as a guide.

One day, on my way to pick up my daughter from her sitter, I thought of how God had been nurturing and guiding me along this journey. Since day one, since birth, He has placed people in my life to get me to the point I am now. Even in the midst of loss, He was still present. I was driving and thinking about how I can be very protective of my daughter. I am so cautious, and I watch her every move. As she began to crawl, I would always follow her, pick her up, and guard her from different items that I felt could hurt her. She would often cry when I took things from her or when I would pick her up from off the floor due to me being afraid that she was trying to pick up objects to put in her mouth or push over items that could hurt her. Her crying let me know that she was not aware that I was protecting her and removing her from potential danger. We often do that with God. We hold on to or continue to move toward what could be detrimental to us because we cannot see what God can see.

As my daughter continues to grow, it is time for her to learn to walk. It is time for her to graduate from crawling. I realized that for this to happen, I had to let her fall at times, even if that meant that she would cry or get slightly hurt. I would be there to ensure that she would not get seriously hurt, of course, but I needed her to be able to learn this skill, so I had to be okay with falls despite her cries. This pain was for her good and her growth. As her mother, I was always right there to guide her, sometimes when she couldn't see me, yet I was always nearby. I was close enough to ensure that if she needed me, I was right there. Is that someone else we know?

God's grace is sufficient in all that we go through. We must be willing to trust Him and utilize His word, using the Bible to help guide us. He has always been near to us, yet we are the ones who remove ourselves from Him. During this journey, I learned that God's love is unconditional. Even during the times, we leave Him, He is right there waiting, yearning for us to allow him to carry the weight. Whether it is the weight of sadness, loneliness, anger, unforgiveness, or hurt, it does not matter. He wants to lessen this burden, but we must allow Him and, again, release control.

During my dark days, God covered me. I was in such deep sorrow that I remember not caring and not wanting to feel better. I felt as if I did feel better or was no longer depressed that I was not showing Damian true love and respect in his time of passing. I did not want to "forget". I refused to heal. Yet, God was patient with me. He knew that my flesh and my spirit were at war. Ephesians 6:12 says, "For we wrestle not against flesh and blood, but against principalities, against powers, against the rulers of the darkness of this world, against spiritual wickedness in high places." I was at war. War with depression, at war with sadness, at war with anger. I was bound and did not know how to get out of this dark hole that I was in. What I soon realized was that God was in this hole with me, waiting to guide me out. I soon decided to take ahold of His hand and allowed Him to lead me.

God was gentle with me, and once He saw that I was willing to surrender to Him and His plan, He guided me to a light that continued to get brighter each day. A life with God is a life of peace, even when you must endure suffering. You know who holds tomorrow, and you know who holds your hand. Once I decided that I wanted to be bolder in God and less in the flesh, I began to see my life change. I started to see life differently. Once again, everything is spiritual. If everything is spiritual, why not increase in spirit? Rise in spirit and lower your flesh. Your flesh is where you lose sight of what truly is. Your flesh can cause you to forget that during trials, God is. God is first. God is last. As my dad would always say if God is Alpha and Omega, meaning first and last, who do you think is in the middle? God. He will never leave you. He is with you always through it all and during all that comes your way. The task at hand is that you trust Him. He will never lead you wrong. Truly knowing that you have a God who is all-knowing and omnipresent, which means he is everywhere, not limited by space and time, is enough to eliminate any worry that creeps into your mind.

If God could protect me and still love me in the midst of the darkness I was in, why would I not devote my time and life to Him? How could I ever not continue to live every day, putting Him first in my life? He has proven once again that His love never fails. 2 Corinthians 12:9, "My grace is sufficient for you, for my power is made perfect in weakness."

Chapter 5

Serenity Prayer: Transformation

I can truly say that a life that is surrendered and given solely to God, is a life full of peace and tranquility. Don't get me wrong, I am not saying that every day will be sunshine and rainbows, but there will be a peace that surpasses all understanding when you know who is in control. As I transform into this new woman along this journey, I realized the more I worry, the more I was doubting God. God has done and continues to do so much for me, how can I and why would I still doubt Him?

I thought back to how Damian proved to me in the beginning that he was a man of his word. After he proved that to me, there was not one time I doubted that he would do what he said. During his celebration of life, I spoke about how if he told me the sky was red, I would have believed him with no doubt, although I had never seen the sky red before. The reason for this type of trust, is because he had proven to me so many times that he was a man of distinction, of honesty and that I had no reason to doubt a man that was such a protector and provider, even when what he said was unfamiliar or out of the norm.

Why is it so hard for us to truly put our trust in God? God often does unexplainable, unrealistic and unimaginable, "out of the norm" things in our lives. When they take place, we do not hesitate to question Him. The creator of all, we question Him. How odd is that? I realize now that the struggle comes when we want to have control over our circumstances. When we cannot "see" where things are going, or when we lack the ability to gain a sense of certainty, we lose trust.

God is not seen in the physical, which is for many of us hard to "trust". We allow our flesh to take over and we forget how to have faith and trust in God all because we cannot "see" God. Cut down your flesh and advance your spiritual eyesight, you will begin to see life in such a different light. Allow God to be present in all that you do. See and feel His presence in everything around you, the good as well as what feels not so good. Allow him to lead and guide you. Know that He is God. Know that He is your protector and will ensure that if you allow Him, He will not take you down a path of destruction. Once you know and truly believe this, is when life will slowly become what it is designed to be, which is an experience and a journey of lessons and blessings. We receive all that God intends for us to have when we trust His will for us. *Read that sentence again.*

His will is so much better than the plan that we wrote down in middle or high school. His will is beyond anything that we could ever imagine. Imagine praying and begging God for a 3-bedroom house with a two-car garage, only for God to have a 5-bedroom, 3 car garage, 2 full walk-in closets, marble countertops, stainless steel appliances and full kitchen waiting for you. Trust, it may not seem that way now, but God is a BIG God, whose plan for us is bigger than what we pray and ask of Him. We are not on a level big enough to even begin to pray for what God truly has in store for us. Allow Him to work. Allow Him to close every door that will lead to better. Allow him to remove what we feel we need. Allow Him to transform by breaking what we feel need fixing or building. Most times what we feel we want or need, God sees differently. Know that His plan is the better plan. We are not equipped to "fix" any problem without His guidance. We are not equipped to make any decision without His direction, so why stress ourselves with trying to do so?

I have often found myself saying, "God, I need you to be clear with me", "I need to know that it is you giving me a sign". We often need it written in plain sight for us to feel as though it is what we should do, or for us to trust. Unfortunately, that is not always the case in life, and it is not always the case with God. If it was that easy, would faith really be "faith"? Simply let go. Simply let God lead you. He has given the roadmap and the blueprint. It is up to us to use it or not. We can try to build without the manual and struggle, or we can utilize the manual and make the outcome better to obtain.

When we receive items such as furniture, or equipment to assemble, they always come with instructions. I am guilty about being in a rush or just sometimes feeling as if "I got this" without reading the instructions or utilizing the manual. Sometimes when taking this route, it takes longer to assemble the item or equipment because I make mistakes, or must redo, take apart and reassemble. If I would have just read the instructions or manual to begin with, I could have avoided this issue and decreased my time that it took to reach the outcome. We do this with life. We are so quick and so eager to "finish", to reach our goals, to get what "we" want, that we forget that God left us a manual and He is also our guide. We try to do so much on our own. One of the biggest mistakes we make in life is leaving God out.

God has proven to me that He will not let me down. Now, there will be times that I do not understand what He is doing, but He is a man that cannot and will not fail. A perfect God. This is proven and said in His word. He is a man that cannot lie. A man that knows all, sees all. What better man to put my trust in?

A full, true relationship with God starts with having faith and trust in Him. Learning that a life being obedient makes it easier to navigate your way through is sometimes desolate to think about. We often look at obedience as "difficult" or forceful. Yet, when you are obedient to God, it helps you be able to avoid so many redoes or dead ends. God wants what is best for us, but remember He gives you free will. We often blame God for a lot of our setbacks, yet do we truly believe that God wants to withhold our blessings? When I think of parenthood, being a mother, I would never want to withhold rewards or accomplishments from my daughter. I want her to receive all that is destined for her. Yet, as she gets older, she can make her own decisions based on what I taught her or have instilled in her. She has free will. My prayer and hope is that she is able to manage what is given and able to understand what comes her way. My prayer is that she utilizes the tools given and know that she has me always, as a guide. The lessons, the talks, the nurturing is all given to help and guide her. I want her to always be able to hear my voice when she needs to make certain decisions, whether she sees my face or not. I want to be imbedded in her heart and able to guide her as she goes throughout life. As a parent I can imagine the hardest thing to watch your child do is self-sabotage or continue to make the same mistakes over again, when if they would only listen and be obedient, trust you as their parent to lead them, they would see that their outcome is so much better. I imagine this same feeling, is what God feels when he watches us be disobedient and often stray away from His will for us. When we want to take control, make our own way and end up hurt or far from where we could be if only, we would trust, surrender and allow Him to be the driving force in our lives.

When you break down the serenity prayer, you will see that it is a prayer of ultimate surrender. Serenity means the state of being calm, peaceful and untroubled. During the loss of Damian, and ultimate pillar in my life. I initially felt turmoil and as if life was full of chaos, hurt and sadness. As soon as I allowed God to completely take control of this situation, a situation that I could not change, I slowly began to feel that "peace that surpasses all understanding". I knew that I could change one thing, and that was allowing God to be the head and giving Him what felt heavy. I no longer wanted to carry this burden, especially knowing that I had the choice not to. I did not have to try to navigate this grief alone. I had the option to allow God to help and guide me or I could continue to be in turmoil and pain. I chose peace. I chose to give it to the one who had ultimate control and accept what had taken place. I chose to allow God to step in, heal my heart, mind and spirit. I chose serenity.

"God grant us the serenity to accept the things we cannot change, the courage to change the things we can, and the wisdom to know the difference.

Amen.

Chapter 6

Let's Evolve

While embarking on this journey to evolve and grow spiritually, I have learned that I have had to cut my flesh deeply. Dying daily sounds scary, but when you think about it, it is essential to die in the flesh daily so that you can be who God wants you to be in Him. The question that we often ask ourselves is, how do you maintain a positive outlook on life when life is not giving you what seems or looks like a positive outcome? Life will undoubtedly throw you curveballs, balls that come at you so fast that it is hard for you to catch or manage them all at once. They will hit you; they will afflict you, and they will hurt.

I came across Psalms 119, verse 71. *It was good for me to be afflicted so that I might learn your decrees.* What if hurt and struggle are truly necessary to become whole? To have the blinders off, to become more intimate with God, to know that He is who He says He is? How would one learn to give Him the weight if the weight is never too hard for them to carry? One does not necessarily utilize their spotter when lifting weights unless it is too heavy for them to lift on their own, right?

Looking back on it all now, without this pain, without the weight of depression, loss, sadness, grief, and uncertainty, I would not have been seeking Him as much as I did. I would not have needed to rest upon Him and allow Him to carry this weight for me. Yes, I have had weight to bear, but again, that was nothing compared to this weight during this journey. I was overburdened. Mentally, physically, and spiritually. I could not carry this weight alone. God, I needed Him like never before. I knew I had nowhere else to turn. I knew that I had to give him this weight to bear. Realizing this was the first way that I had evolved.

I was evolving spiritually through pain, and I did not know it at the time. When the tunnel is dark, it is hard to see that there is light at the end. The only way to learn and to see the light is to keep going. The light becomes more and more visible the more we force ourselves out of the darkness. My dad would once tell a story of a young woman and her father riding through a storm. The young girl was driving, her father on the passenger side. As she was driving through the storm, she told her father that she could not see and that she felt as though she needed to pull alongside the road. Her father said, "You must keep going; you will soon be out of the storm. If you stop now, you will just prolong getting through it". The young girl continued driving through the storm until soon she was out of the storm, and there were clear skies. Her father then told her to pull alongside the road. The young girl was confused because she was now out of the storm and could see clearly. Her father told her to look behind her so that she could see

48

where she had come from and through. He said, "See, if you would have stopped back there in the storm, you would not be here, in the clear. You would still be back there in the storm".

There is no way around heartache and pain in this life. There will be hardships and trials if we are in this world—the world of sin. We often feel as though it is not fair that to grow, we must endure pain. As we look at the great influences of today, many of them have great stories. Stories of trials, tests, and lessons that they have had to learn to be who and where they are today. God uses broken people. Being broken gives you a battle wound, a scar. According to the Merriam-Webster dictionary, a scar is defined as a mark remaining (as on the skin) after injured tissue has healed. There is a scar, which means yes, you were once hurt, once wounded, punctured, or attached, but you are now healed. Sometimes, it takes a while for the scar to appear, meaning it takes time for one to recover. A scar usually occurs after a significant puncture, not usually after something minor. It is okay to have scars that come with life. These scars allow you to remember how far you have come, yet most importantly, it qualifies you to be one to tell others just how the grace and awe of God are transparent in all of our lives. A scar is a symbol that you are chosen for this and chosen to live on and tell your story.

During my season of being broken, I knew that the only place I had to go at this time was up. I chose to evolve. I decided not to allow my situation to leave me stuck there. In life, remember you have free will. Choose wisely. What is interesting about growing in faith, in God, and in spirit is that you began to focus on what your purpose or lesson is during the storm instead of solely focusing on the storm. You push through and allow God to sit with you as you travel through the storm.

At the beginning of my brokenness, the start of this journey, I felt so much anger. I only wanted to know "Why me?", 'How could God do this to me?". I never once sat and thought, "What does God need me to see?" "What is the lesson in this?" "What level is God trying to get me to reach spiritually". I had not yet evolved. I was not there yet. I lacked the knowledge, strength, and intimacy that God wanted of me. Yet, He knew. He knew that during this test, this trial, I would soon evolve and learn just what He intended all along.

It was all necessary to reach the next phase. It was all required for me to evolve and see with a clearer mind, an open heart, and my spirit, not flesh. The scales lifting from your eyes are when you finally see God is with you in the struggle. He is with you and will help you not only get through but grow through, help you to evolve. You will not and should not be the same person at the end of the test.

As a student who goes to the next grade level, they must first master their current level. To master their current level, they will be tested. They will have quizzes; some may be pop quizzes. They will have assignments to complete, and they will have to study. It is truly a journey to earn the reward at the end.

I recently attended my younger cousin's high school graduation. As an honor graduate receiving scholarships and awards and the most important achievement, his diploma, I know that he had to pass tests, assignments, and quizzes. He put in the work and did not stop even if times were hard, even if he may have become frustrated.

As a woman of God who is and has evolved, I had to pass the test. I had to complete the assignment given to me. It was not easy, and to continue growing, I am sure there will be other assignments. Each level requires a new test and a new assignment. The difference is that now, as I grow spiritually, I no longer want to be the one to question "why." It is essential to seek the lesson that is set in front of you to learn. Evolving is developing gradually and growing from a simple to a more complex form. Challenge your spirit to evolve. Diminish, cut, and continue to allow your flesh to die daily so that you can then see what God's will is for your life. What does God want you to see? Who does He need you to guide and help along the way because of your story and the journey that you were chosen to take?

Genesis 37-50 talks about the story of Joseph. Joseph is an excellent representation of what is said regarding all things working together for the good of those who love the Lord, which is in Romans 8:28. Joseph was sold by his brothers as an enslaved person and was purchased by a captain of the guard of Pharaoh. Yet, even as an enslaved person, Joseph turned every experience and every circumstance, no matter how difficult or hurtful, into something good. Evolving spiritually is the ability to do just that. Even in heartache, in death, in loneliness, in sickness, in overall trying times, allow yourself to seek and see God. Let's evolve and continue to have the ability to turn everything into something good. When we do this, this is a godly characteristic that shines through you. I call it "God's Glow".

Chapter 7

Fullness: Fill me up, God.

For I know the plans I have for you, declares the Lord. Plans to prosper you and not to harm you, plans to give you hope and a future. Jeremiah 29:11.

We believe that we have our life all planned out. We usually start at a very young age by picturing and planning the life that we want and hope to have for ourselves. We go as far as having timelines and wishing to complete a specific task by a certain age or timeframe. I have learned in my years on this earth that it is an excellent and positive idea to "plan." It keeps you organized and on track and gives you a visual representation of your goals. Yet, they are just that, "your" goals. Things change, life changes, and you must be ready for that to happen. It could come out of nowhere, or you could have the opportunity to prepare for change, yet change is inevitable. The good thing about change is that once you have mastered the understanding that God's plan is better than your plan, living based on His will, and began to lean on the scripture Jeremiah 29:11, peace will be upon you as you rest upon the unknowing of life's journey.

Life's journey is entirely of uncertainty. When you think you may have it all figured out, you realize you have so much more to learn. As spoken numerous times before, everything is spiritual. God's plan always supersedes what we feel is needed or wanted in our lives. A wise woman, Apostle Dr. Deborah Sheppard, once told me, "We are not smart enough to navigate this life without God." This is a very true statement that provided me with insight into the fact that I should always consult God and listen and watch for His guidance along this journey. He wants to give us our desires, yet we must understand that we must pray that our desires align with His will. Read that sentence again.

We are so quick to say, "God will give us the desires of our heart," but do we pray and ask God to create in us a clean heart and renew within us the right spirit? Do we pray that He gives us what He wants for us and allows us to live by His will? Many times, we are not willing to be uncomfortable and face the hard truths. We are not willing to allow God to prune us and open our eyes to what we "thought" we wanted. Yet, for us to receive all that God wants to give and for us to live according to His will, we must be willing to give up the things that are out of His will. God cannot fill or overflow a basket with beautiful, sweet fruit if you are carrying a basket that has a few rotten fruits in it. Do you know what happens to a ripe, lovely, beautiful piece of fruit if it is around a rotten fruit? Yes, it becomes rotten as well. You must be willing to clean out your basket (your heart, soul, and spirit) if you want God to send in the overflow of blessings.

Pruning and asking God to reveal is not always a great feeling. As a matter of fact, it usually is a painful experience. It is almost like detoxing the body. Many of us are familiar with detoxing our bodies from bad foods or drinks. We know how hard it is to stop eating sweets or go on a diet that consists of healthier options. The first couple of days or weeks are hard. We even feel inadequate at times. Yet, as time goes on, we start to feel better than ever. We began to see the great benefits. We have clearer skin, more energy, a healthier weight, and we even think more clearly. Well, detoxing and cleaning spiritually is just as essential and honestly more critical. We fill our spirit with so much "junk" and wonder why we cannot hear God. We wonder why it feels as if our blessings are being "held up" by God. The question is, are we ready for the blessings? Are we able and equipped to handle what God has in store for us? You cannot grow when you are confined in a tight space when your mind and spirit are limited. Many of us operate at low frequency. We have not been able to hear, see, or grow in the way that we would like because we are bogged down by the many chains that we refuse to get free of.

It is essential to search deeply within ourselves. Many times, we are not where we want to be because we have some detoxing to do. Ask yourself, "Am I in covenant with anything that is not pleasing in the eyesight of God?" Honestly, you could be like me and not honestly know the answer to this question right away.

Yet, the Holy Spirit will guide you and lead you in the direction that you need to go. Never underestimate those "random feelings" that you get when you are around, in, or about to do certain things. It all leads back to what has been stated often in this book, "everything is spiritual." The random signs, the random people that come into your life that give you a message that seems to convict you or a message that resonates so much with you.

We must be spiritually fit and spiritually fed that we are consuming what will bring us closer to God, not away. We are already in a world of sin, so the best way to navigate this life while we are here is to operate in a way that we are not only in a solid relationship with God but in a way that we are of high spiritual enlightenment that we can also be intercessors for others. The prayer is to be fulfilled by God and fulfilled in all that God has for us—allowing God to help us rid ourselves of what is holding us back. We often hold tight to what we currently have when God has something so much better. To grow, we must expand. We see how, for a home, building, or space to be developed, contractors or construction workers have to more than likely tear down the current walls and rebuild. Allow God to expand, fill you up with quality material, and allow Him to upgrade your space and your heart.

Being fulfilled by what God has for you is a feeling that gives you the satisfaction that you often search in the wrong places for. We usually chase this feeling of being fulfilled or complete. The reason many of us feel so incomplete is because we lack the fulfillment of God. We lack what He has and wants to give us. Once we are filled with God, our other blessings come into our lives and accentuate the joy that was already there. God is literally living water. He fills us and gives us life. God gives a refreshing feel to our thirst. Our spirit longs to be quenched. We must be filled and allow God to continue to pour into us. It is imperative to be filled with God's love and grace to have a life that is prosperous in all areas. In the Bible, Jesus talks about drinking water in John 4:13-14. Jesus answered, "Everyone who drinks this water will be thirsty again, but whoever drinks the water I give him will never thirst." The difference between the water and the well that he was referring to is that water can and may soon run dry. What Jesus gives is eternal life; it is not stagnant; it forever flows through us. This water is living water, the Holy Spirit. God comes to live in us through the Holy Spirit. Our deepest desire and longing is to be closer and more like Jesus. It should fulfill us and give us the joy that we search for. I am by no means saying that we should not desire what many of us do, such as family, a great career, wealth, marriage, children, friends, and perfect health, just to name a few. I am simply saying that our deepest desire should be to allow God to enter into our lives and fill us with His "living water." By allowing this, we will learn that the yearning and the "impatience" or lack of understanding of how God is moving in our lives will be replaced with the peace and contentment the Holy Spirit comforts us with. That anxiety and sense of urgency is a bondage that must be broken. "Whoever comes to me will never be hungry again. Whoever believes in me will never be thirsty again". John 6:35

I have and continue to be filled with God's living water. When I slowly began to detox spiritually, I was able to make room, expand, and grow in spirit. By all means, it was not easy, and I still find days where I struggle to manage and understand what direction to go. The one constant thing that keeps me grounded is the river that flows forever—the daily walk through the power of the Holy Spirit. I want to continue to fill my cup because by doing so, I find myself refreshed, revived, and reborn.

"You provide the fire; I'll provide the sacrifice. You provide the spirit, and I will open inside. Fill me up, God, fill me up, God, Fill me up, God". -Tasha Cobbs

Biography

Born to Pastor Kenny and Azzie Gouch on July 7, 1992, in Americus, GA. I grew up in the small town of "Garden valley, GA. The oldest of two girls. My younger sister is Kenyatta Gouch who has given me a niece, Khloé Davis. I graduated high school in 2010 from Macon County High School and continued my education at Fort Valley State University. I graduated with a Bachelor of Social Work in 2014 and decided to go back to Fort Valley State University to obtain my Master of Public Health, which I completed in 2017. I have over 10 years of experience in Child Welfare and Human Services. In 2022 I opened a Child Placing Agency, Bridge Builders Family and Children Services. I am also a program manager for the Air Force. I am a mother of one daughter, Nia Jai Gouch-Todd. I am my daughter, sister, mother, friend, business owner, corporate employee, survivor and now author.

Made in the USA
Columbia, SC
24 December 2024

48425020R00033